Flying
PUMPKINS!

Rob Waring, *Series Editor*

HEINLE
CENGAGE Learning

Australia • Brazil • Japan • Korea • Mexico • Singapore • Spain • United Kingdom • United States

Words to Know

This story is set in the United States. It happens in the state of Delaware.

—Delaware

 A Contest. Read the paragraph. Label the pictures with the correct form of the <u>underlined</u> words.

This story is about an unusual competition, or contest, between various teams. The winner in this contest is the team that throws a <u>pumpkin</u> farther than anyone else. The teams use different types of equipment and machines to throw the pumpkins. Some teams use a <u>catapult</u> to throw their pumpkin. Some teams use a <u>cannon</u> to blow their pumpkin through the air. One team even uses <u>garage door springs</u> and a kind of container called a <u>bucket</u> to get their pumpkin to fly. Before the contest, teams practice throwing many different things. They throw <u>watermelons</u>, <u>kegs</u>, and even <u>refrigerators</u>!

1. _____

2. _____

3. _____

B Weights and Measures.

Weights and Measures. In the story you will read about pounds to measure weight and feet to measure distance. What are these weights and distances in metric measures?

> **1 pound = .45 kilograms**   **1 foot = .31 meters**

1. 8 pounds = _____ kilograms

2. 387 feet = _____ meters

3. 1,728 feet = _____ meters

4. _____

5. _____

6. _____

7. _____

8. _____

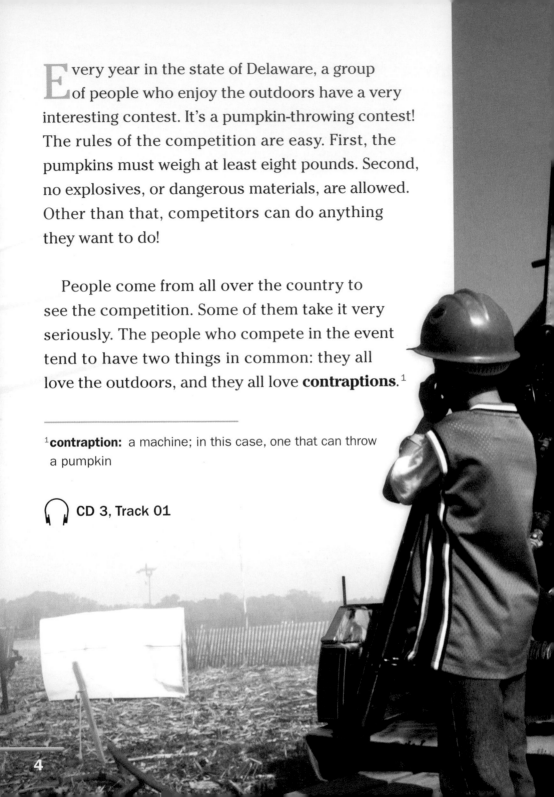

Every year in the state of Delaware, a group of people who enjoy the outdoors have a very interesting contest. It's a pumpkin-throwing contest! The rules of the competition are easy. First, the pumpkins must weigh at least eight pounds. Second, no explosives, or dangerous materials, are allowed. Other than that, competitors can do anything they want to do!

People come from all over the country to see the competition. Some of them take it very seriously. The people who compete in the event tend to have two things in common: they all love the outdoors, and they all love **contraptions**.[1]

---

[1]**contraption:** a machine; in this case, one that can throw a pumpkin

CD 3, Track 01

There are several teams that take part in the contest. Mick Davies is part of a group which has been coming to the contest for many years. Mick talks about his team, and how they've gotten better since they began. "We started out with a little contraption with about 14 garage door springs on it," he says. "We threw 387 feet that first year— and we've progressed from there."

So what do they call this strange contest that keeps people coming back year after year?

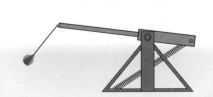

A Pumpkin-Throwing Contraption

This fun annual contest's unusual name is the **'Punkin' Chunkin'**[2] Contest.' The aim of the contest is simple: to make a machine that can throw a pumpkin through the air. The machine that throws—or chunks—a pumpkin the farthest wins. The teams make these contraptions themselves. They work hard to make original machines that will chunk a pumpkin a long way.

Some women compete in the event, but not many. However, the contest does affect the men's wives—especially while the men prepare for the Punkin' Chunkin' Contest. One team member explains, "The ladies that don't like to get involved, they know right around September...October, that [it's] about time to become a Punkin' Chunkin' **widow**."[3]

---

[2]**Punkin' Chunkin':** [pʌŋkɪn tʃʌŋkɪn] pumpkin throwing

[3]**widow:** a woman whose husband is dead; here the man means a woman whose husband is never around because he's busy preparing for the contest

The unusual sport of Punkin' Chunkin' began over 20 years ago. In those days, there were only three teams and a few friends who came to watch. But now, more than 20 years later, this strange contest has really grown. It's become very popular. Today, the contest attracts more than 80 teams, and more than twenty thousand people come to watch it!

Fact Check

1. Where does the contest happen?

2. What is the contest called?

3. What is the goal of the contest?

4. When did it start?

In Punkin' Chunkin', the actual sport itself is not that difficult. However, people have to think carefully about the design of the machine if they want to win. All of the teams in the contest think that they've created just the right one. John Huber is a member of a team named 'Team Hypertension.' He talks about their machine: "It's probably one of the few machines on this field that's really **engineered**,[4] so that we know **what it can take**[5]—every bit of it." He goes on to say, "I know what every **weld**[6] can hold. There isn't anything that's going to surprise us."

Team Hypertension started seven years ago. It used garage door springs to throw its first pumpkin from a bucket. Since that time, the competition has become much more advanced.

---

[4]**engineer:** design or create something according to scientific methods
[5]**what it can take:** how much the machine can do
[6]**weld:** a part where metal is joined to metal

Nowadays, Punkin' Chunkin' machines can be anything from a simple catapult to an actual cannon. A good design isn't everything, though. If a team really wants to win, they need to practice. To do this, they throw many things, not just pumpkins. A member of one team explains: "We chunk pumpkins, watermelons, kegs, toilets, refrigerators, **microwaves**,[7] tires ... we chunk anything we can **get our hands on**!"[8] Unfortunately, even with a lot of practice, things don't always go perfectly. Accidents can still happen!

---

[7]**microwave:** an electric tool for cooking that uses waves of energy to cook or heat food quickly

[8]**get (one's) hands on:** *(slang)* find; be able to use

Predict

**Answer the questions. Then, scan page 17
to check your answers.**

1. One year, a team had an accident. What
   kind of accident did the team have?

2. In the accident, they 'took out a vendor'.
   What do the words 'vendor' and 'take
   out' mean?

One year, a team destroyed a vendor's table with their pumpkins!

One 'Punkin' Chunker' tells the story of an accident that happened at one of the contests. During the competition, his team tossed, or threw, their pumpkins backwards! "We tossed two backwards last year. We actually **took out**[9] one of the **vendors'**[10] tables; there was a coffee table, and [we] just kind of destroyed it," he says.

---

[9]**take out:** break; destroy
[10]**vendor:** seller of food, drinks etc.

It's not just the pumpkins that break sometimes. This year, Team Hypertension's pumpkin is very big and it breaks part of their machine. Luckily, despite this difficulty, their machine throws a pumpkin over 1,728 feet! Team Hypertension wins the contest again. After the event is over, John Huber happily announces, "The King of Spring is still **in charge**!"[11]

The event is over for another year. But if you happen to be in Delaware at the right time, remember to look up to the sky. You just may have your own chance to see a real flying pumpkin!

---

[11]**in charge:** the boss or leader

After You Read

1. What is one of the rules of the Delaware pumpkin contest?
   A. No explosives are allowed.
   B. Pumpkins must weigh at least ten pounds.
   C. People must be serious.
   D. The contest is in the spring.

2. In paragraph 1 on page 6, the word 'it' means:
   A. a pumpkin
   B. a spring
   C. the outdoors
   D. the contraption

3. The winner is the machine that throws the _____.
   A. closest
   B. farthest
   C. biggest
   D. shortest

4. Around what time of year is the Punkin' Chunkin' Contest?
   A. July and August
   B. August and September
   C. September and October
   D. October and November

5. Who are 'the men' in 'the men's wives' on page 9?
   A. men who don't like chunkin'
   B. men who can't join the contest
   C. men who eat pumpkins
   D. men who join the contest

6. On page 10, the word 'strange' in 'strange contest' means:
   A. terrible
   B. unusual
   C. boring
   D. great

7. How many people watch the contest nowadays?
   A. more than 20,000
   B. more than 80,000
   C. less than 20,000
   D. 20,000

8. The most important part of the throwing machine is the:
   A. size
   B. design
   C. weight
   D. color

9. Which was NOT listed as a practice item for throwing?
   A. refrigerators
   B. watermelons
   C. toilets
   D. sofas

10. On page 17, what two things were thrown backwards?
   A. pumpkins
   B. vendors' tables
   C. coffee tables
   D. kegs

11. Why is the 'King of Spring' still the leader?
   A. because his team won for the first time
   B. because everybody knows him
   C. because his team won again
   D. because his machine is the most famous

12. What is the main purpose of this story?
   A. to show how far pumpkins can fly
   B. to introduce an unusual hobby and event
   C. to explain that catapulting is hard
   D. to share part of Delaware's culture

CENTRAL HIGH
NEWSPAPER

TENTH GRADERS WIN CATAPULT

Every year the students of Central High School study European history, and every year, there is one subject in which students are always very interested. They all love learning about the strange contraptions that ancient cultures used to fight their wars. One of the most interesting of these contraptions is the catapult. Long ago, invaders used this machine to throw huge rocks against the walls of castles. If the machine worked correctly, the rocks broke the wall. This allowed the fighters to enter the castle. These ancient catapults were usually heavy wooden contraptions.

Invaders Attacking an Ancient Castle with Catapults

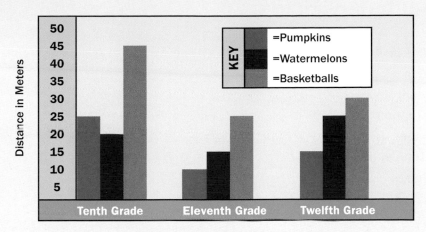

Catapult Competition Results 2008

Due to student interest in this ancient method of attack, the history department at Central High started the catapult competition ten years ago. Every year, teachers and students from the art, science, and history departments spend months planning and researching. Everyone works together and attempts to build catapults that work very well. Then, students in grades ten, eleven, and twelve actually compete against each other to see who can throw the farthest. However, instead of throwing rocks, Central students throw pumpkins, watermelons, and basketballs. The team that throws these objects the farthest, wins.

Everyone learns a lot from building the machines, and the competition itself is always very fun. Hundreds of friends and family members always attend.

This year, the tenth graders surprised everyone by winning the competition. The results of the competition have been included in the graph above. As you can see, the tenth-grade group did especially well with the basketball throwing. One reason that the tenth graders may have won is because they studied the science of catapults carefully. They discovered that the arm of the catapult needs to be very long. They also realized that the machine has to be very heavy so that it stays still when it's used. Even though the tenth graders had the least experience building catapults, they did an excellent job. Good work everybody!

CD 3, Track 02

Word Count: 322
Time: _____

Vocabulary List

bucket (2, 13)

cannon (2, 14)

catapult (2, 14)

contraption (4, 6, 7, 9)

engineer (13)

get (one's) hands on (14)

in charge (18)

keg (2, 14)

microwave (14)

pumpkin (2, 4, 7, 9, 13, 14, 16, 17, 18)

refrigerator (2, 14)

spring (2, 6, 13, 18)

take out (15, 17)

vendor (15, 16, 17)

watermelon (2, 14)

weld (13)

what it can take (13)

widow (9)